Messianic Haggadah

(for use with "Observing the Feast of Passover - An Eternal Ordinance)

Written by

Messianic Rabbi Allan Moorhead
Messianic Rabbi Gil Kaplan
Messianic Rabbi Fern Marcy

Copyright 2016 by Hebraic Harvest International, Inc.
All Rights Reserved.

Copyright © 2016 Hebraic Harvest International. United States of America All Rights Reserved under international copyright laws. Contents and/or cover may not be reproduced in whole or in part without prior written consent of Hebraic Harvest International.

Printed in the United States of America

Published by Aion Multimedia
20118 N 67th Ave
Suite 300-446
Glendale AZ 85308
www.aionmultimedia.com

ISBN-13: 978-0-9976046-2-7

All scripture quotations, unless otherwise indicated, are taken from the Tree of Life Bible, Copyright © 2015 by The Messianic Jewish Family Bible Society. Used by permission.

Scripture quotations marked (KJV) are taken from the King James Bible, New York: American Bible Society: 1999.

Scripture quotations marked (CJB) are taken from The Complete Jewish Bible, An English Version of the Tanakh and B'rit Hadasha. Clarksville, Md: Jewish New Testament Publications, 1998.

"Bedikas Chametz being performed on 2009-04-07" by Rabbi Moish Soloway, https://commons.wikimedia.org/wiki/File:BedikasChametz.jpg. License at https://creativecommons.org/licenses/by-sa/3.0/legalcode

"Lord's Table" by John Snyder, https://commons.wikimedia.org/wiki/File:Lord%27s_Table.JPG#filelinks. License at https://creativecommons.org/licenses/by-sa/3.0/legalcode.

"Passover Table 2" by April Killingsworth, https://www.flickr.com/photos/aprillynn77/11515727. https://creativecommons.org/licenses/by-sa/2.0/legalcode.

"Matzah" by Paurian, https://www.flickr.com/photos/paurian/127502681/. License at https://creativecommons.org/licenses/by-sa/2.0/legalcode.

"Horseradish" by Anna Reg,
https://commons.wikimedia.org/wiki/File:Kren_Verkauf.jpg. License at
https://creativecommons.org/licenses/by-sa/3.0/legalcode.

"Kiddush-Cup-and-Saucer" by Yoel Ben-Avraham,
https://www.flickr.com/photos/epublicist/9242981484. License at
https://creativecommons.org/licenses/by-nd/2.0/legalcode.

"Judaica Kiddush Cup" by Shalom Gurewicz,
https://www.flickr.com/photos/70682325@N00/5285701491
License at https://creativecommons.org/licenses/by/2.0/legalcode

Table of Contents

Transliteration Key

An aid to pronunciation of Hebrew words

a or ah	a as in father
ai	i as in kite
e or eh	e as in bet
ee	ee as in beet
ei or ey	a as in late
i	i as in big
o	o as in bold
u	oo as in tooth
ch	ch as in Bach

Hebrew Terminology

Adonai - LORD יהוה (YHVH)
Afikomen - dessert, comes from Greek for 'I Came'
Beytzah - Egg
Chag Sameach - Happy Holiday
Chametz/Hametz - Leaven
Charoset - Apple mixture
Dayenu - It would have been enough
Haggadah - The Telling; book used to follow Passover Seder
Hallel - Praise
Halleluyah - Praise the LORD
HaMashiach - The Messiah
Hillel - an ancient rabbi before Yeshua
Karpas/Karpos - Greens
Kiddush - Sanctification
Korech - Combine
La Shana haba ah - The year to come
Mah Nishtana - What makes this night different?
Maror - Bitter Herb
Matzah - Unleavened Bread
Mo'edim - Appointed Times
Nirtzah - Desire
Nisan - 1st month of biblical calendar
Racht'zah - Washing Place
Seder - Order; The traditional full dinner event
Shabbat - Sabbath, the 7th day of the week (52 each year); any Holy Convocation specified in Leviticus (7 each year)
Talmidim - Disciples
Torah - First five books of the Bible, often referred to as Books of Moses; The Law
Urchatz - Wash hands
Yachatz - Breaking in half
Yerushalayim - Jerusalem
Yeshua - Jesus
Z'roah - Lamb Bone

The Passover Seder - The Haggadah

The Hebrew word *Seder* means "order". This definition indicates the service has a particular order. The Hebrew word *Haggadah* means "the telling". *Haggadah* is the booklet name used to tell the Passover history and is a valuable tool for sharing this information with future generations.

The specific food items used for Passover are determined by scripture. Exodus 12:8 tells us that roasted lamb, matzah (unleavened bread) and Maror (bitter herb) are required to observe Passover. Because there is no longer a temple in which to conduct the sacrifice and roast the lamb, a lamb bone serves as a symbolic replacement. Other food items are traditional and help to further illustrate the symbolism of this event and its implications for believers.

Scripture also tells us that Yeshua/Jesus celebrated Passover and during this celebration and its rituals that the Lamb of God made the atoning sacrifice on our behalf— for salvation and deliverance. All of this and more will be revealed and explained in detail as we go through the Seder service. Enjoy your Passover Seder, and on behalf of all of us, we wish you a *Chag Sameach* (Happy Holiday)!

The Passover Table

Passover Table 2

The Seder begins with everyone gathered at a beautifully set table. When a large group is celebrating together, if possible, seat the leader(s) at a head table to lead the service.

On the table you will find the following special Passover items:

- Set of candlesticks.
- A ceremonial wine glass for each person to use for blessings throughout the Seder.
- A small bowl of salt water - symbolizing the tears of the Hebrew slaves.
- Our Seder table is completed by a bowl of water and small towel for ceremonial hand washing.
- Additional place setting, usually set in a prominent place, with a special wine goblet, referred to as the "Cup of Elijah".
- A special platter (called a Seder Plate) which holds the biblical and traditional elements.

The Biblical items are:

- Z'roah – Lamb Shank - representing the Passover lamb.
- Maror – Bitter Herb - representing the hardships endured as slaves. Horseradish is typically used.
- Matzah - Unleavened Bread - representing affliction and haste in leaving Egypt.

The Traditional Items are:

- Charoset – made of chopped apples and nuts, mixed with sweet wine, honey, and cinnamon - representing the mortar for the bricks made for Pharaoh's cities.
- Karpas – Parsley - representing life, symbolized by the color green.
- Beytzah – Roasted egg - a custom which began during the Babylonian captivity and represents the Passover sacrifice. It also symbolizes the mourning for the destruction of the temple and the inability to offer sacrifices.
- Chazeret - Some plates have a place for a second type of bitter herb which may be used in the Hillel Sandwich.

Additionally, a small pillow may be on the leader's chair, indicating the easier life we now lead after our deliverance from "bondage", which is another expression for the sin of the world we live in. "However, now, freed from sin and enslaved to God, you do get the benefit - it consists in being made holy, set apart for God, and its end result is eternal life" (Romans 6:22 CJB).

Preparing Ourselves For Passover

Removal of Leaven

In preparation for the Feast of Passover and the Feast of Unleavened Bread (which begins the following day), all leaven is to be removed from the home (Ex 12:15). According to Exodus 12:19-20, no food containing yeast or leaven, called Chametz, is to be found in the house or consumed during the Feast of Unleavened Bread. In scripture, leaven or yeast is often symbolic of sin, wickedness, evil, and false doctrine. While removal of the physical leaven from our homes is paramount during this season, the removal of spiritual leaven from our lives should be an ongoing activity. How do we remove sin from our lives? We seek the Messiah, and acknowledge our sin by confessing it. We repent by changing our behavior and turning back to the will of God. Then will we see the glorious work of the Lord in our lives.

What an awesome concept – knowing that we can come before Yeshua and repent because “He has removed our sins from us as far as the east is from the west” (Psalm 103:12 CJB).

1 Corinthians 5:6-8 says, *“Your boasting is no good. Don’t you know that a little hametz leavens the whole batch of dough? Get rid of the old hametz, so you may be a new batch, just as you are unleavened—for Messiah, our Passover Lamb, has been sacrificed. Therefore let us celebrate the feast not with old hametz, the hametz of malice and wickedness, but with unleavened bread—the matzah of sincerity and truth.”*

Scripture declares that we are all sinners.

Ecclesiastes 7:20 says, *"Surely there is not a righteous person on earth who does what is good and doesn't sin."*

Romans 3:23 states, *"for all have sinned and fall short of the glory of God."*

Sin separates us from God.

Isaiah 59:2 declares, *"Rather, your iniquities have made a separation between you and your God. Your sins have hidden His face from you, so that He does not hear."*

Sin brings death.

Ezekiel 18:20a (CJB) reads, *"The person who sins is the one that will die..."*

Romans 6:23 says, *"For sin's payment is death, but God's gracious gift is eternal life in Messiah Yeshua our Lord."*

Luke 13:3b (CJB) says, *"...unless you turn to God from your sins, you will all die as they did!"*

Atonement for sin requires a blood sacrifice and repentance.

Leviticus 17:11 declares, *"For the life of the creature is in the blood, and I have given it to you on the altar to make atonement for your lives—for it is the blood that makes atonement because of the life."*

1 Peter 1:18-19 reads, *"You know that you were redeemed from the futile way of life handed down from your ancestors—not with perishable things such as silver or gold, but with precious blood like that of a lamb without defect or spot, the blood of Messiah."*

Yeshua the Messiah was punished for all our sin.

Isaiah 53:5, 6b, and 12b declares, *"But He was pierced because of our transgressions, crushed because of our iniquities. The chastisement for our shalom was upon Him, and by His stripes we are healed... So Adonai has laid on Him the iniquity of us all...For He bore the sin of many, and interceded for the transgressors..."*

God is the only one who can remove our sins.

Isaiah 1:18 declares, *"'Come now, let us reason together,' says Adonai. 'Though your sins be like scarlet, they will be as white as snow. Though they be red like crimson, they will become like wool.'"*

The LORD in Isaiah 43:25 says, *"I, I am the One who blots out your transgressions for My own sake, and will not remember your sins."*

1 John 1:7 promises, *"But if we walk in the light as He Himself is in the light, we have fellowship with one another and the blood of His Son Yeshua purifies us from all sin."*

And finally, 1 John 1:8-9 adds, *"If we say we have no sin, we are deceiving ourselves and the truth is not in us. If we confess our sins, He is faithful and righteous to forgive our sins and purify us from all unrighteousness."*

Good deeds and removal of physical leaven from our houses cannot remove sin.

Isaiah 64:6 (KJV) says, *"But we are all as an unclean thing, and all our righteousnesses are as filthy rags;"*

Ephesians 2:8-9 reads, *"For by grace you have been saved through faith. And this is not from yourselves—it is the gift of God. It is not based on deeds, so that no one may boast."*

We must realize that removal of leaven is only symbolic. We should strive daily to inspect and clear our spiritual house (ourselves) of any and all sin. In many strict Orthodox Jewish homes, the physical leaven found is only swept up and thrown away or burned. However, we as believers in Yeshua, through confession of our sins to Him, our sins are destroyed…so that we will not have the "sin" to return to.

An interesting custom in some Jewish circles is to “sell” the leaven to someone else who is unaware of the biblical commandment. Then the leavened products are bought back after the feast is over. This action allows a person or business to honor God’s instruction to remove leaven without suffering economic repercussions. This may work well in the natural. The questions is: “What is the spiritual implication of having someone else take on your sin, and then asking for it back?

Search for Leaven

There is a Jewish tradition of searching for the leaven. Since the leaven has already been removed from the home, a small amount of bread or crumbs are left in a conspicuous place for the "search".

Bedikas Chametz being performed on 2009-04-07

Before beginning the Seder, the family will indulge in an extensive search of the household for this chametz, usually involving the children. In preparation for the search, the family gathers with a lit candle (just as the light of our Messiah will reveal any sin that might still be left in our lives).

A wooden spoon and feather are used to sweep up any leftover leaven. The wooden spoon represents the execution stake of the Messiah and the feather represents a dove, which in turn symbolizes the Holy Spirit.

As a parent carries a lit candle, the children are able to find the few crumbs and participate by sweeping it up and throwing it away. By participating, our children learn a wonderful lesson about the removal of sin from their lives.

This holds significance for us as believers. Leaven (or chametz) represents sin. Using the light of Yeshua, the atonement from his blood sacrifice and by the power of the Holy Spirit we should search within ourselves to remove all traces of sin.

The following blessing is recited before the leaven is searched for:

בָּרוּךְ אַתָּה יְיָ אֱלֹהֵינוּ מֶלֶךְ הָעוֹלָם אֲשֶׁר קִדְּשָׁנוּ
בְּמִצְוֹתָיו וְצִוָּנוּ עַל בִּעוּר חָמֵץ

LEADER: Baruch atah Adonai Eloheynu Melech ha'olam a'sher kid'shanu b'mitz-vo-tav v'tzee-vah-nu al bee-ur chametz. Amen.

ALL: Blessed are You, O LORD our God, King of the Universe, Who has sanctified us with Your commandments, and instructed us concerning the removal of leaven. Amen.

(A family searches for, finds, and sweeps up the crumbs.)

Celebrating the Passover and Our Deliverance!

As we continue with our service, we can all begin to relive the experience of physical bondage and deliverance that the Hebrews went through. We also begin to understand how Yeshua brought us true spiritual liberation and redemption.

The woman of the house will light the candles and lead us in the following blessings.

(Light the candles.)

The Candle Lighting Blessing

בָּרוּךְ אַתָּה יְיָ אֱלֹהֵינוּ מֶלֶךְ הָעוֹלָם אֲשֶׁר קִדְּשָׁנוּ בִּדְבָרֶךָ

וְנָתַן לָנוּ אֶת יֵשׁוּעַ מְשִׁיחֵנוּ וְצִוָּנוּ לִהְיוֹת אוֹר לְעוֹלָם

FEMALE LEADER: Baruch atah Adonai Eloheynu Melech ha'olam asher kid'shanu bid-varecha v'natan lanu et Yeshua Mishicheinu v'tzee-vah-nu l'hee-ote ohr l'olam. Amen.

ALL: Blessed are You, O LORD our God, King of the Universe, Who has sanctified us by Your Word and given us Yeshua our Messiah, and commanded us to be a light to the world. Amen.

The Sh'Hecheyanu: A Traditional Blessing for Special Occasions

בָּרוּךְ אַתָּה יְיָ אֱלֹהֵינוּ מֶלֶךְ הָעוֹלָם שֶׁהֶחֱיָנוּ וְקִיְּמָנוּ

וְהִגִּיעָנוּ לַזְּמַן הַזֶּה

FEMALE LEADER: Baruch atah Adonai Eloheynu Melech ha'olam, sh'hecheyanu, v'kee-manu v'higianu lazman hazeh. Amen.

ALL: Blessed are You, O LORD our God, King of the Universe, who has kept us alive, sustained us, and brought us to this time. Amen.

Kiddush - The Cup of Sanctification - The First Cup

Sanctification means, "to be set apart or made holy."

When God first made the covenant with Abraham, all of Abraham's descendants (through Isaac) were set apart. Let's consider this: When the Children of Israel first came to Egypt, they were given the land of Goshen. Even though they were later enslaved, they were still set apart.

Even today's Believers, both Jew and Gentile, are set apart by the sanctification of the Holy Spirit because, like Abraham, their faith is counted as righteousness.

This first cup represents our acknowledgement of being chosen and set apart, as children of the most High God.

LEADER: Let us lift our first cup together and bless the Lord.

בָּרוּךְ אַתָּה יְיָ אֱלֹהֵינוּ מֶלֶךְ הָעוֹלָם בּוֹרֵא פְּרִי הַגָּפֶן

LEADER: Baruch atah Adonai, Eloheynu Melech ha'olam, borey p'ri hagafen. Amen.

ALL: Blessed are You, O LORD Our God, King of the Universe, Who creates the fruit of the vine. Amen.

(Take the first sip from the cup. Leave the rest for additional blessings throughout the Seder.)

Urchatz - Hand Washing

So far, we have been set apart and sanctified - made Holy. As we continue our journey, we must continually maintain this state. This is done through cleansing. *Urchatz* comes from the Hebrew word *Rachatz* meaning “washing”.

One derivative of Rachatz is *Rach-tzah* meaning “a washing place”. In a way, this symbolizes the purification of the priests at the brazen laver. The priests were required to wash their hands and feet at the brazen laver before entering the Tabernacle.

Exodus 30:20-21 (CJB) explains, *“when they enter the tent of meeting - they are to wash with water, so that they won't die. Also when they approach the altar to minister by burning an offering for ADONAI, they are to wash their hands and feet, so that they won't die. This is to be a perpetual law for them through all their generations.”*

This was an act of repentance and of the filling of the Holy Spirit. The brazen laver was made from polished brass mirrors of the Hebrew women. The idea of seeing yourself in a mirror is a repentance concept because we are to see ourselves as we really are. Water also symbolizes the Holy Spirit. We must understand that cleansing is a major part of preparation before entering the Holy Place, as well as ministering to and meeting with the LORD.

As we wash, we realize that the work of the Holy Spirit and our faith in Yeshua is what cleanses us.

John 13:4-5 reads, *"So He gets up from the meal and lays aside His outer garment; and taking a towel, He wrapped it around His waist. Then He pours water into a basin. He began to wash the disciples' (Talmidim) feet, drying them with the towel wrapped around Him."* This act of our Messiah gives a beautiful example of humility as well as service to one another!

בָּרוּךְ אַתָּה יְיָ אֱלֹהֵינוּ מֶלֶךְ הָעוֹלָם אֲשֶׁר קִדְּשָׁנוּ בְּמִצְוֹתָיו

וְצִוָּנוּ עַל נְטִילַת יָדָיִם

LEADER: Baruch atah Adonai, Eloheynu Melech ha-olam, asher kid'shanu b'mitz-vo-tav v'tzee-vah-nu al netilat y'dayim. Amen.

ALL: Blessed are You, O LORD Our God, King of the Universe, Who has sanctified us by Your commandments and commanded us regarding the washing of hands. Amen.

Now let us pass the bowl of water to each other and conduct this ceremonial washing by dipping our fingers and drying them with the towel.

Karpas/Karpos - Parsley

This symbolic ceremony was not part of the original Passover observance. The dipping of parsley was added by the rabbis around the 11th century. Its procedure evolved into the dipping as we know it today.

An early rendition represented dipping Joseph's wool coat into animal's blood to suggest to his father Jacob that he had been killed. This would introduce the events that led up to the Israelites coming to Egypt. A later version, which we observe today, relates the end of the story where renewal and new life overcome the hardships of slavery.

The Greek word *Karpos* means "fresh raw vegetable" but the Hebrew word *Karpas* means "fine white linen. *Karpas* is found in only one place in the Bible and that is in Esther 1:6 which is translated as "green" in the King James Bible. More than likely the writer of the book of Esther probably meant fine white linen and blue hangings in the King's palace and not blue and green hangings.

With that in mind, let's consider what we have done so far in our Seder. We have removed the sin (leaven) from our lives by the grace and forgiveness that comes by way of Yeshua's sacrifice. We have cleansed ourselves at the special washing place, thus being refreshed and filled with the Holy Spirit. And now we don the fine white linen of the biblical priests, as we prepare to minister to the Lord.

The parsley is a reminder of spring - the season of Passover. It is a green plant of the earth, representing life. The salt water represents the tears of all those enslaved. By dipping the parsley into the salt water we are encouraged that, even through our tears of hardship and trials, renewal of abundant life is available through the salvation of our Messiah.

John 16:33 says, *"These things I have spoken to you, so that in Me you may have shalom. In the world you will have trouble, but take heart! I have overcome the world!"*

Dip the parsley in the salt water and hold it while the blessing is recited.

בָּרוּךְ אַתָּה יְיָ אֱלֹהֵינוּ מֶלֶךְ הָעוֹלָם בּוֹרֵא פְּרִי הָאֲדָמָה

LEADER: Baruch atah Adonai, Eloheinu Melech ha'olam, borey p'ri ha'adamah. Amen.

ALL: Blessed are You, O LORD our God, King of the Universe, Who creates the fruit of the earth. Amen.

(Eat the parsley.)

Yachatz - Divide in Half: Breaking the Middle Matzah

On each table, there is a set of three matzot —or three large pieces of unleavened bread. They can be found in a divided packet called a Matzah Tosh (Unity Bag) or on a designated matzah plate separated by napkins. The matzot are together, or united, yet they are separated into three different compartments.

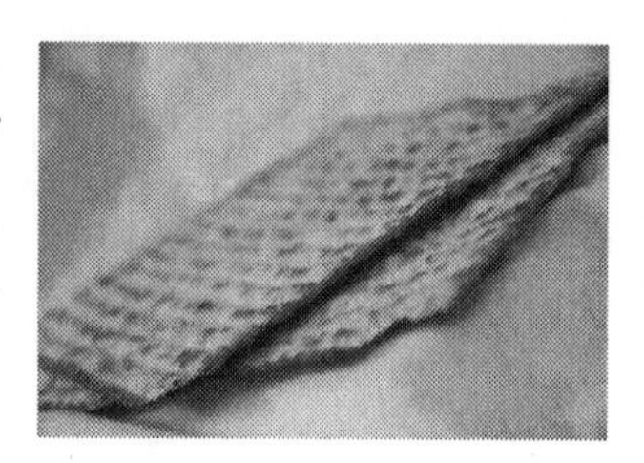

Matzah

The matzot are used in the ceremony of dividing in half, or "*yachatz*", where the middle matzah is broken in two. One half is returned to the middle position and the other half will be hidden. The portion which will be hidden is called the "Afikomen." This will be described in more detail later.

Now let's break the middle matzah in half and put one piece back in the middle. The remaining piece is wrapped with a white linen napkin and set aside for later. We wrap this half to symbolically "bury" it.

(This linen wrapped piece will be hidden by the leader of the head table during the dinner break for the children's search later in the Seder.)

Amazingly, this ceremony of "*Yachatz*" with three pieces of matzah is done in Jewish homes around the world without true understanding of the significance and meaning of it.

There are various explanations by the rabbis as to why there are three matzot for this portion of the Seder. Some ancient rabbis agree that it is a symbol of unity representing Abraham, Isaac, and Jacob. Many say it represents the Priests, the Levites, and the people of Israel. With either of these rabbinic explanations for this tradition, the question is... Why would Isaac or the Levites be taken out and broken in half, wrapped in linen, and hidden?

There is, however, ONE unity that fits perfectly in this situation: the Father, the Son, and the Holy Spirit. Just as the Afikomen was wrapped and hidden away, Yeshua (the Son)'s bruised body was wrapped for burial and hidden from sight.

This is described in Mark 15:46. *"Joseph bought a linen cloth, took Him down, wrapped Him in the linen, and laid Him in a tomb that had been cut out of the rock. Then he rolled a stone against the door of the tomb."*

We see the matzah as a representation of deliverance and freedom that Messiah Yeshua bought for us with His sacrifice. The sinless Yeshua (the unleavened bread) was buried on the evening of the first day of Unleavened Bread, a high Sabbath. *"The Jews therefore, because it was the preparation, that the bodies should not remain upon the cross on the sabbath day, (for that sabbath day was an high day,) besought Pilate that their legs might be broken, and that they might be taken away."* (John 19:31 KJV).

Consider the Matzah

Have you ever noticed the way matzah looks today? It is striped and pierced and without leaven. Can this be a reflection of the Son, Yeshua, whose body was striped and pierced and He had no sin?

Psalm 22:17 declares, *"For dogs have surrounded me. A band of evildoers has closed in on me. They pierced my hands and my feet."*

Isaiah 53:5 says, *"But He was pierced because of our transgressions, crushed because of our iniquities. The chastisement for our shalom was upon Him, and by His stripes we are healed."*

Zechariah 12:10 (KJV) reads, *"And I will pour upon the house of David, and upon the inhabitants of Jerusalem, the spirit of grace and of supplications: and they shall look upon me whom they have pierced, and they shall mourn for him, as one mourneth for his only son, and shall be in bitterness for him, as one that is in bitterness for his firstborn."*

John 19:34 records, *"But one of the soldiers pierced His side with a spear, and immediately blood and water came out."* and in verse 37 *"And again another Scripture says, 'They shall look on Him whom they have pierced.'"*

Maggid - Telling the Story of Passover: From Affliction to Abundance

The Bread of Affliction

Because there arose a pharaoh who did not know Joseph, the Hebrews were enslaved for many years and endured much hardship. The Bread of Affliction - matzah made with only wheat and water - reinforced the concept of humiliation and suffering. In contrast, we have also seen how the matzah is a representation of deliverance and freedom that Messiah bought for us with His sacrifice.

As we share and partake of the matzah, we begin our transition out of the "slave" mentality. We were once slaves, now we are free. In our freed state, we now begin to share. May all who are needy come and celebrate the Passover with us. May all who are hungry come and eat. Revelation 22:17 (CJB) expresses, *"The Spirit and the Bride say, 'Come!' Let anyone who hears say, 'Come!' And let anyone who is thirsty come - let anyone who wishes, take the water of life free of charge."*

ALL: May Adonai's appointed people, known as Israel, speedily come to know His fullness and that all may be satisfied in the knowledge and understanding of the Messiah.

Ma-Nishtanah - What is Different (about this Night)?

LEADER: *"When your children ask you, 'What do you mean by this ceremony?'"* (Exodus 12:26 CJB)

It is our responsibility to pass on to each new generation the story of the wonders and miracles that show the glory and the might of our God. As our children ask what is different about this night, they point out four specific observances referred to as "The Four Questions". This provides the opportunity for us to share this event from history as well as express who the Almighty God is and how faithful He is to His people. These questions are traditionally asked by the youngest child who is able to recite them.

HEBREW: (read by the child)

מַה נִּשְׁתַּנָּה הַלַּיְלָה הַזֶּה מִכָּל הַלֵּילוֹת

Mah nishtanah halailah hazeh mikol haleylot?

שֶׁבְּכָל הַלֵּילוֹת אָנוּ אוֹכְלִין חָמֵץ וּמַצָּה הַלַּיְלָה הַזֶּה כֻּלּוֹ מַצָּה

Shebechol haleylot anu ochleen chametz umatzah. Halailah hazeh kulo matzah?

שֶׁבְּכָל הַלֵּילוֹת אָנוּ אוֹכְלִין שְׁאָר יְרָקוֹת   הַלַּיְלָה הַזֶּה
מָרוֹר

Shebechol haleylot anu ochleen she'ar yerakot.   Halailah
hazeh maror?

שֶׁבְּכָל הַלֵּילוֹת אֵין אָנוּ מַטְבִּילִין אֲפִילוּ פַּעַם אֶחָת
הַלַּיְלָה הַזֶּה שְׁתֵּי פְעָמִים

Shebechol haleylot eyn anu matbileen afilu pa'am echat.
Halailah hazeh shtey f'ameem?

שֶׁבְּכָל הַלֵּילוֹת אָנוּ אוֹכְלִין בֵּין יוֹשְׁבִין וּבֵין מְסֻבִּין
הַלַּיְלָה הַזֶּה כֻּלָּנוּ מְסֻבִּין

Shebekol haleylot anu ochleen beyn yosh-veen uveyn mesubeen.
Halailah hazeh kulanu mesubeen?

ENGLISH: (read by the child)

Why is this night different from all other nights?

On all other nights we eat bread or matzah. On this night we eat only matzah?

On all other nights we eat all kinds of vegetables. On this night, we eat only bitter herbs?

On all other nights, we do not dip even once. On this night we dip twice?

On all other nights we eat our meals sitting up or relaxing. On this night we all relax together?

ALL: The phrase *Mah Nishtana* more specifically means "What has changed?" Tonight we remember that our ancestors were slaves in Egypt under Pharaoh. Yet it all changed according to Deuteronomy 26:8: "Then Adonai brought us out from Egypt with a mighty hand and an outstretched arm, with great terror, and with signs and wonders."

LEADER: Consider what would have happened if God never responded to the cries of the people while enslaved. Would the children of Israel have become a nation and brought forth the richness of our Messiah? This turning event shows us that God **IS** faithful in His promises. Through His original faith covenant with Abraham, He brought us from slavery to a life of fulfillment with a new covenant of being God's people as He declares Himself to be our God. It is a story of God's love, justice, and care – for those whose hope is in Him.

The matzah reminds us of the haste in which our ancestors left Egypt, for the dough had not the time to rise. We must be ready to move as the LORD instructs. Our preparations may not be able to fully develop (or rise like the bread), but moving at the LORD's command will result in His glory and our redemption and deliverance.

The maror reminds us of the bitterness of the bondage of slavery which the Hebrews experienced under Pharaoh. We remember also our bondage of sin before our Messiah, the Passover Lamb, delivered us from the slavery of sin.

We dip matzah twice on this night – the first time (Matzah and Bitter Herb) as a symbol of hardship and bitterness of bondage; and the second time (Matzah, Bitter herb, and Charoset) to sweeten the taste of that bitterness, knowing that even in the bitter times of life, Yeshua is our joy, strength, and sweetness.

Relaxing is an act of the free man who can eat in leisure. The pillow reminds us of our freedom. For in trusting God, we are secure.

The Exodus

The story of the Exodus actually begins with one of Jacob's sons named Joseph, who was highly loved and favored. Joseph's brothers were jealous and betrayed him. They told Jacob that Joseph was killed by a wild animal. This nearly broke Jacob's heart. The brothers sold Joseph into slavery and he ended up in Egypt. Later, Joseph was falsely imprisoned. However, God was continually watching after him.

"The Exodus of the Israelites from Egypt" by David Roberts

Eventually, because of Joseph's interpretations of Pharaoh's dreams, he was released from prison and immediately raised to second in command over all of Egypt.

Joseph's leadership, decisions, and actions saved Egypt and the surrounding nations from starvation during a severe famine. Joseph's father, Jacob, and his brothers came to Egypt during this time of famine and were reunited with Joseph. Their entire household numbered 70 and they were given homes in the lush pasture land of Goshen. There, they lived for many years and prospered.

430 years later, the original 70 Hebrews grew into hundreds of thousands. A Pharaoh arose that did not know of Joseph or recall how he saved Egypt. He became fearful of the large number of Hebrews so he enslaved them and killed their male babies to keep the Hebrews from increasing any further.

However, through divine protection, a male baby was spared. He was found and raised by Pharaoh's daughter. His name was Moses. Eventually, Moses learned of his heritage. He slew an Egyptian for beating a Hebrew, then Pharaoh sought to kill him. So Moses fled to the land of Midian. While in the land of Midian, he met the LORD. God called out to him from a burning bush and revealed that He would use Moses to bring His people out of Egypt.

Along with his brother, Aaron, Moses followed God's instructions in dealing with Pharaoh. Even so, God said in Exodus 3:19-20, "*Nevertheless, I know that the king of Egypt will not let you go, except by a mighty hand. So I will stretch out My hand and strike Egypt with all My wonders that I will do in the midst of it. After that, he will let you go*." True to God's word, Pharaoh refused to let the Hebrews go. So God sent judgment in the form of plagues on Egypt. Pharaoh would give permission for the Hebrews to leave, and repeatedly changed his mind. It took ten plagues, the tenth being the death of all of the firstborn in Egypt, before Pharaoh finally decided to let the Hebrews go.

During the entire time of this judgment, God protected the Hebrews from many of the plagues, especially the final plague: the death of the first-born. The Hebrews followed God's commands concerning this plague and they were passed over by the Angel of Death during the judgment of God on Egypt.

In obedience to God's command, the Hebrews took an unblemished male lamb of the first year and observed it for four days in their own homes.

On the 14th day of the Hebrew month of Nisan, the whole assembly of the congregation of Israel was to kill their lambs in the evening. The blood of each household lamb was to be placed on the upper and side doorposts of each house. That night, God came to slay all of the first-born. If He saw the blood, He "passed over" that house and all who were in the household were spared. Thus the name Passover was established.

As we continue with our observance, one can just imagine what it was like that night, when the Angel of Death came. The Hebrews must have heard the wailing of the Egyptian families as the first born of both men and beasts died, as they themselves were huddled together trusting in God for their safety because of the Blood of the Lamb.

Today, God's judgment passes over those who have correctly appropriated the blood of Messiah Yeshua; of whom John the Immerser was referring to when he said "Behold the Lamb of God."

When we accept this atonement of the Messiah, His blood is placed on the doorposts of our hearts, and the judgment of God passes over us. By the strength of His own arm, He redeems all who call upon Him. The Messiah gave His life for us on the 14th of Nisan as the

Passover lambs were being offered. He is the ultimate Passover Lamb.

1 Peter 1:18-19 relates, *"You know that you were redeemed from the futile way of life handed down from your ancestors—not with perishable things such as silver or gold, but with precious blood like that of a lamb without defect or spot, the blood of Messiah."*

After the tenth and final plague, which was the death of the firstborn, Pharaoh let the Hebrews go. He soon changed his mind and pursued the Hebrews, only to see his army drown when trying to chase the Hebrews across the Red Sea. God had delivered the Hebrews from a mean, stubborn Pharaoh. The children of Israel became a free people, a new nation.

ALL: The Exodus of the Hebrews from Egypt serves as an example for everyone today of the exodus from our bondage of sin. As the Hebrews were delivered by the blood of a lamb, so today we are delivered by the blood of the Lamb of God.

As the Hebrews received their baptism in the Red Sea (1 Corinth 10:2, KJV, *"And were all baptized unto Moses in the cloud and in the sea"*), today we receive our baptism through the Holy Spirit. As the Hebrews were promised a land of milk and honey, today we are promised eternal life.

Let us not be like Pharaoh and resist the will of God in our lives. It can only bring suffering.

Obedience to God will bring the blessings and prosperity of the Law of God. Yes, the Law of God is still in effect today. Yeshua said, *"Amen, I tell you, until heaven and earth pass away, not the smallest letter or serif shall ever pass away from the Torah until all things come to pass*" (Matthew 5:18).

In fact, Yeshua said, *"Whosoever therefore shall break one of these least commandments, and shall teach men so, he shall be called the least in the kingdom of heaven: but whosoever shall do and teach them, the same shall be called great in the kingdom of heaven"* (Matthew 5:19, KJV).

According to Yeshua, it is important to be obedient to the commandments of God. When we don't obey the commandments of God, we have to remember that according to scripture, we are required to repent. So we have to ask ourselves, "What are we to repent for?" Sin, of course. What is sin? It is violation of God's commandments. So the commandments still apply to all of mankind even today.

Makkot - The Cup of Plagues - The Second Cup

Egypt was facing the judgment of God. The Egyptian gods could not protect them. The God of Abraham, Isaac, and Jacob demonstrated that He is the one true God. Even Pharaoh's magicians acknowledged this. They were able to duplicate the first two plagues. However, they were NOT able to duplicate the next. Exodus 8:15 relates, "*So the magicians said to Pharaoh, 'This is the finger of God.'*"

Yet we do not rejoice in the Egyptian calamities. Psalm 23:5 says, "*You prepare a table before me in the presence of my enemies. You have anointed my head with oil, my cup overflows.*" Our cup runs over with the fullness and joy of the Lord, but now we must diminish this full cup in remembrance of the judgment of God against Pharaoh and Egypt.

As we recite each plague, let us dip our clean little finger into the cup and allow a drop of liquid to fall upon our napkin. Just as the wine in our cup is diminished, so too is the joy of deliverance reduced by knowing the terrible price that was paid.

1. Blood
2. Frogs
3. Lice (gnats)
4. Beasts
5. Cattle disease
6. Boils
7. Hail
8. Locusts
9. Darkness
10. Death of the firstborn

(The cup remains on the table.)

The First Plague: Water Is Changed into Blood, watercolor by James Tissot

The Third Plague of Egypt: Gnats (Exodus 8:17) by William de Bralies

The Seventh Plague: John Martin's painting of the plague of hail and fire (1823).

DAYENU means "It would have been enough for us". This is a traditional song sung on Passover, praising God for His overwhelming kindness and faithfulness. Let us praise God for doing more than enough.

DAYENU - It Would Have Been Enough For Us

(To be sung in Hebrew. Translation in italics)

Ilu hotzi hotzi onu
Hotzi onu mi Mitzrayim (repeat) Dayenu
(If He had brought us out of Egypt, it would have been enough)
Dai dayenu, dai dayenu, dai dayenu, dayenu dayenu
Ilu notan notan lanu
Notan lanu et ha Shabbat (repeat) Dayenu
(If He had given us the Sabbath, it would have been enough)
Dai dayenu, dai dayenu, dai dayenu, dayenu dayenu
Ilu notan notan lanu
Notan lanu et ha Torah (repeat) Dayenu
(If He had given us the Torah, it would have been enough)
Dai dayenu, dai dayenu, dai dayenu, dayenu dayenu
Ilu notan notan lanu
Notan lanu et Yeshua (repeat) Dayenu
(If He had given us Yeshua, it would have been enough)
Dai dayenu, dai dayenu, dai dayenu, dayenu Dayenu

Hallel

Let us now recite Psalm 113 and praise the Lord!

ALL: Halleluyah!

Praise, O servants of Adonai, praise the Name of Adonai.

Blessed be the Name of Adonai from now and forever.

From the rising of the sun to its going down the Name of Adonai is to be praised.

Adonai is high above all nations, His glory is above the heavens.

Who is like Adonai our God, enthroned on high,

who brings Himself down to look upon heaven and upon earth?

He raises the poor from the dust, lifts up the needy out of the dunghill,

to seat him with princes, with the princes of His people.

He settles the barren woman in her home as a joyful mother of children.

Halleluyah!

LEADER: We now lift the cup and recite the blessings.

בָּרוּךְ אַתָּה יְיָ אלֹהֵינוּ מֶלֶךְ הָעוֹלָם בּוֹרֵא פְּרִי הַגָּפֶן

LEADER: Baruch atah Adonai, Eloheinu Melech ha'olam, borey p'ri hagafen. Amen.

ALL: Blessed are You, O LORD our God, King of the Universe, Who creates the fruit of the vine. Amen.

(All take a second small sip.)

ALL: At the appointed time, the Messiah came. He delivered us from another "Pharaoh" and set us free. He is the light of the world, the living water. He loves us, protects us, cares for us, and has made us kings and priests in His name. He gave us the Holy Spirit to be with us until He returns. We are forever grateful. Bless the Lord.

Rach-Tzah - The Washing Place

We have moved from a place of judgment into deliverance. We honor and praise God for doing more than we really deserve. Let us go to the washing place and cleanse ourselves again. As we now prepare to partake of the biblical elements referenced in Exodus 12:8, we shall again recite the blessing and "wash our hands".

בָּרוּךְ אַתָּה יְיָ אֱלֹהֵינוּ מֶלֶךְ הָעוֹלָם אֲשֶׁר קִדְּשָׁנוּ
בְּמִצְוֹתָיו וְצִוָּנוּ עַל נְטִילַת יָדַיִם

LEADER: Baruch atah Adonai, Eloheynu Melech ha-olam, asher kid'shanu b'mitz-vo-tav v'tzee-vah-nu al netilat y'dayim. Amen.

ALL: Blessed are You, O LORD our God, King of the Universe, who has sanctified us by Your commandments and commanded us regarding the washing of hands. Amen.

LEADER: Although there is no biblical commandment to wash our hands before we eat, we do so to remind ourselves that our hearts must be clean before the Lord. As we symbolically wash our hands, we, spiritually, are once again sanctified by the Holy Spirit in order to minister to the Lord with the passover elements.

Psalm 24:3-4 (KJV) reminds us, *"Who shall ascend into the hill of the Lord? or who shall stand in his holy place? He that hath clean hands, and a pure heart; who hath not lifted up his soul unto vanity, nor sworn deceitfully."*

So as you dip your fingers, consider your relationship with the LORD and ask for forgiveness if needed.

Pass the bowl, dip and dry your fingers.)

Motzee Matzah - Bring Forth the Matzah

The matzah (unleavened bread) was one of the three foods commanded to be eaten in Exodus 12:8.

Matzah

At this time each guest is to receive a medium sized piece of matzah which is taken from the upper or top matzah and the remaining half of the middle matzah.

בָּרוּךְ אַתָּה יְיָ אֱלֹהֵינוּ מֶלֶךְ הָעוֹלָם הַמּוֹצִיא לֶחֶם מִן הָאָרֶץ

LEADER: Baruch atah Adonai, Eloheynu Melech ha'olam, ha'motzi lechem min ha'aretz. Amen.

ALL: Blessed are You, O LORD our God, King of the Universe, Who brings forth bread from the earth. Amen.

בָּרוּךְ אַתָּה יְיָ אֱלֹהֵינוּ מֶלֶךְ הָעוֹלָם אֲשֶׁר קִדְּשָׁנוּ בְּמִצְוֹתָיו וְצִוָּנוּ עַל אֲכִילַת מַצָּה

LEADER: Baruch atah Adonai, Eloheynu Melech ha'olam, a'sher kid'shanu b'mitz-vo-tav v'tzee-vah-nu, al achilat matzah. Amen.

ALL: Blessed are You, O LORD, our God, King of the Universe, Who has sanctified us by Your commandments and commanded us to eat unleavened bread. Amen.

(Everyone take a small bite of matzah.)

Maror - Bitter Herb

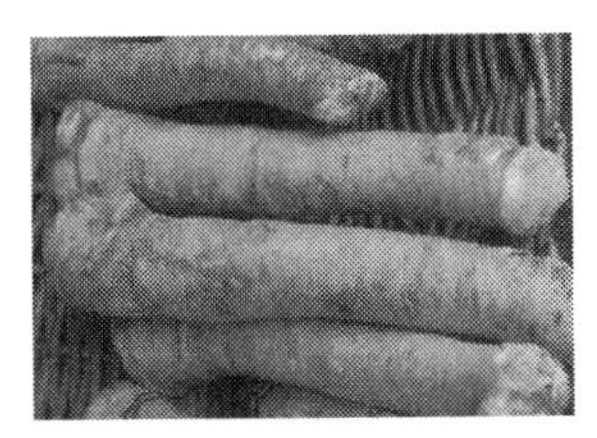
Horseradish

On Passover, we are commanded to eat bitter herbs. Let us never forget the bitterness felt by the Children of Israel who were in bondage in the land of Egypt. After we dip the Matzah into the Maror, we will recite the blessing and then eat it. We let its bitter taste bring tears to our eyes, as compassion enters our hearts for those who also suffer in bondage and oppression.

בָּרוּךְ אַתָּה יְיָ אֱלֹהֵינוּ מֶלֶךְ הָעוֹלָם אֲשֶׁר קִדְּשָׁנוּ
בְּמִצְוֹתָיו וְצִוָּנוּ עַל אֲכִילַת מָרוֹר

LEADER: Baruch atah Adonai, Eloheynu Melech ha'olam, asher kid'shanu b'mitz-vo-tav v'tzee-vah-nu al achilat maror. Amen.

ALL: Blessed are You, O LORD Our God, King of the Universe, Who has sanctified us by Your commandments and commanded us to eat bitter herbs. Amen.

(Everyone partakes of the maror.)

As a side note: At Yeshua's Last Seder, He identified Judah (Judas) as the one who would betray Him as they participated in this tradition. John 13:26a reads, *"Yeshua answers, 'It's the one I will give this bit of matzah to, after I dip it'..."* Judas' betrayal was indeed bitterness to Yeshua.

We Dip Twice - Charoset

"On all other nights we don't even dip once, but on this night we dip matzah twice."

A traditional ritual that is observed in Jewish homes during the second dipping is known as *korech* meaning "combine".

A generation before the time of Yeshua, one of the great rabbis from history, Rabbi Hillel, initiated the practice of combining matzah, bitter herbs, and a bit of the Passover lamb offering. This was to honor the scriptural command that "They shall eat it upon unleavened bread and bitter herbs." As the end of temple sacrifices took away the opportunity to consume the roasted lamb referenced in scripture, a lamb bone is now displayed on the seder plate as the representation of the roasted lamb. This custom of combining the biblical elements has more recently been replaced by what is commonly referred to as the Hillel Sandwich: a piece of matzah, dipped in bitter herbs then dipped in charoset, and then covered with another piece of matzah.

Charoset is the sweet apple mixture rabbis have added to the seder elements. This chunky mixture has traditionally symbolized the wet mortar and straw that the Hebrews used to make bricks while slaves in Egypt. The charoset is now used as a substitution for the lamb in order to carry on the tradition of combining the elements.

Everyone should now put some bitter herbs and charoset between two pieces of matzah in sandwich fashion. As we eat the Hillel sandwich, it should remind us that even bitter circumstances are sweetened by the great joy, liberation, and redemption we have in Messiah Yeshua, our Lord and Savior.

(Make and eat your Hillel sandwich.)

This concludes the first portion of the Seder and it is customary to break for Dinner at this point.

(During Dinner, the leader of the head table hides the Afikomen - the wrapped piece of matzah.)

Resume the Seder

LEADER: The Bible speaks to us in Exodus 12:46 concerning the Passover lamb, *"It is to be eaten inside a single house. You are not to carry the meat out of the house, nor are you to break any of its bones."* Numbers 9:12 also says, *"They are not to leave any of it until morning, or break any bones. When they celebrate Passover they are to observe all its regulations."*

The significance of this is that each family is to consume the lamb or burn the remainder before morning. Exodus 12:10 states *"So let nothing of it remain until the morning. Whatever remains until the morning you are to burn with fire."* Neither are we to carry any portion of it outside of our house. The spiritual understanding here is that we are to totally consume every aspect of Yeshua our Messiah. We can't pick and choose what we want of Him or from Him. It's all or nothing! Nor can we live off of another's relationship with the Messiah. Each and every one of us needs Him personally in our lives.

Another important fact is that when Yeshua was on that execution stake (cross), none of His bones were broken either, although the two criminals with Him had their legs broken.

Yeshua's body was bruised for us from beatings, whips, and other abuses, yet no bone was broken in fulfillment of the scriptures concerning the Passover lamb. Isaiah 53:7 says, *"He was oppressed and He was afflicted yet He did not open His mouth. Like a lamb led to the slaughter, like a sheep before its shearers is silent, so He did not open His mouth."*

Yes, as John the Immerser said, "Behold the Lamb of God."

The Afikomen - Tzafun - Hidden

Remember, the Afikomen is that piece of matzah which was broken, wrapped, and hidden away. This represents the death and burial of our Lord Yeshua.

The word *Afikomen* comes from the Greek language. It is a form of the Greek word *Ikneoma*, which means "I came". YES...Yeshua came, and will come again.

In temple times, the lamb was the last thing eaten when celebrating Passover. This was so that the taste of the lamb would linger to remind us of the great deliverance. Today the Afikomen is the last thing to be eaten. It is referred to by many as "Dessert". Certainly, since finding and redeeming the Afikomen represents His resurrection, it should be the longest lasting taste and greatest thought in our minds.

This taste of matzah reminds us that Yeshua is the "Bread of Life" and it is a memorial to us for our great deliverance from sin and death. We are forever grateful for His sacrifice because He loved us so much.

Now, the children have the chance to search for the Afikomen which was hidden earlier. The one who finds it may receive a small gift. This is considered the reward for redeeming the Afikomen.

Now the Afikomen will be brought forth symbolizing His resurrection. As the children excitedly search for the Afikomen, let us also search for and receive every aspect of Yeshua into our lives with the same excitement.

(Children search for the Afikomen. The child that finds it receives a small reward.)

As the children rejoice in finding the Afikomen, let us rejoice in the discovery of Yeshua and all He represents.

The Lord's Supper: New Covenant Passover

We now come to "The Lord's Supper." This represents the final Passover Seder meal Yeshua celebrated with His disciples before He went to lay down His life for us.

Lord's Table

At this point, the Table Leader will remove the Afikomen from its "Burial Cloth" and break it into pieces and distribute it to each of the guests.

As we partake of the Afikomen, we realize that it was at this point of Yeshua's celebration of the Seder that He instituted what is known as the Lord's Supper (New Covenant Passover or Holy Communion) as a perpetual memorial, fulfilling the meaning of Passover.

He is the Living Bread that came down from Heaven, given for us. With His blood, He purchased our freedom from sin and death. Let this be a time of contemplation, when we search our hearts for any sin in our lives; and for recommitting ourselves to keeping God's ways before we partake of the Lord's Supper, so that we do not "eat and drink in an unworthy manner" (1 Corinthians 11:27).

The partaking of the Afikomen is more than likely the point at which Yeshua, in Matthew 26:26 as they were eating the Seder meal, took the bread (Matzah), blessed and broke it, and gave it to the disciples and said, "take, eat, this is My body."

In 1 Corinthians 11:23-24, because the Corinthians had violated the spirit and purpose of the Lord's Supper in an unworthy manner, the Apostle Paul gave the model way in which to partake of it and says the following: *"For I received from the Lord what I also passed on to you—that the Lord Yeshua, on the night He was betrayed, took matzah; and when He had given thanks, He broke it and said, "This is My body, which is for you. Do this in memory of Me."*

And so we do this now, remembering that this is the matzah which commemorated, throughout the history of Israel, the Exodus out of Egypt and is one of the three foods commanded to be eaten in the Bible. Exodus is now brought to full meaning by Yeshua as His body was bruised for us.

Let's all eat of our piece of Afikomen Matzah with a heart of thanksgiving.

(Partake of the Afikomen.)

Ha Ge-ulah - The Cup of Redemption - The Third Cup

As we lift the cup for the third time, we understand that it has traditionally been a cup of celebration for the freedom and deliverance that comes from God. We believe that this was the cup Yeshua lifted when He said in Matthew 26:27-29 (CJB), *"Also he took a cup of wine, made the b'rakah, and gave it to them, saying, 'All of you, drink from it! For this is my blood, which ratifies the New*

Covenant, my blood shed on behalf of many, so that they may have their sins forgiven. I tell you, I will not drink this `fruit of the vine' again until the day I drink new wine with you in my Father's Kingdom.'"

Then, in 1 Corinthians 11:25-26, the Apostle Paul says it this way: *"In the same way, He also took the cup, after supper, saying, 'This cup is the new covenant in My blood. Do this, as often as you drink it, in memory of Me.' For as often as you eat this bread and drink this cup, you proclaim the Lord's death until He comes."*

ALL: LORD, we understand that Your word tells us that without the shedding of blood there is no remission of sin (Hebrews 9:22). Your precious blood was poured out for us. We are now justified by the shedding of Your blood and receive the gift of eternal life, and thus escape Your wrath.

Thank you for the opportunity to draw near to You, LORD, by the covering of Your blood, the blood of Messiah. Because of the chastisement upon You, we now have peace. We are so grateful for what You have done. Thank You, LORD, in the name of our Messiah and Lord, Yeshua.

בָּרוּךְ אַתָּה יְיָ אֱלֹהֵינוּ מֶלֶךְ הָעוֹלָם בּוֹרֵא פְּרִי הַגָּפֶן

LEADER: Baruch atah Adonai, Eloheynu Melech ha'olam, borey p'ri ha'gafen. Amen.

ALL: Blessed are You, O LORD our God, King of the Universe, Who creates the fruit of the vine. Amen.

(Take a third small sip.)

Birkat Hamazon - Blessing After the Meal

We have now completed the natural meal (Dinner & Seder Elements) and the spiritual meal (New Covenant Passover). Let us now bless the LORD for His provision.

ALL: Blessed are you, O LORD, our God, King of the Universe, creator of time and space, who feeds the entire world through Your goodness, with mercies that endure forever. And by Your great goodness, never shall we be, in need. Great is the glory of Your name.

The Place of Elijah

Kiddush-Cup-and-Saucer

Malachi 3:23-24 says, *"Behold, I am going to send you Elijah the prophet, before the coming of the great and terrible day of Adonai. He will turn the hearts of fathers to the children, and the hearts of children to their fathers—else I will come and strike the land with utter destruction."*

It was prophesied that Elijah would return to prepare the way for the Messiah. Malachi 3:1 says, *"'Behold, I am sending My messenger, and he will clear the way before Me. Suddenly He will come to His Temple —the Lord whom you seek— and the Messenger of the covenant —the One whom you desire— behold, He is coming,' says Adonai-Tzva'ot."* So, it is believed that Elijah would be this messenger. We also know that John the Baptist, also known as Yochanan the Immerser, came in the spirit of Elijah.

John was indeed the messenger described in Malachi 3:1 as stated by Yeshua in Luke 7:27, *"This is the one about whom it is written, 'Behold, I send My messenger before You, who will prepare Your way before You.'"* John came in the spirit of Elijah, yet Elijah himself will return some day.

A special place is prepared at the table in anticipation of Elijah's coming. Will he come this year? It is customary for a young child to go to the main door of the home, open it, and see if Elijah has arrived.

(Child looks for Elijah at the front door)

As we open the door to seek the messenger, we say...

ALL: Come Elijah, with word of our returning Messiah.

ELIYAHU - Elijah (To be sung)

Eli-ya-hu ha na-vi, Eli-ya-hu ha tish-bi

Eli-ya-hu, Eli-ya-hu, Eli-ya-hu ha Gil-a-di

Bim-hey-ra b'ya-mey-nu, Ya-a-vo e-ley-nu

Im Ma-shi-ach ben-Da-vid,

Im Ma-shi-ach ben-Da-vid

LEADER: Elijah the prophet, Elijah the Tishbite, Elijah the Giladite, may he soon come to us with Messiah, Son of David.

Hallel - The Cup of Praise - The Fourth Cup

After the meal, we drink a cup of praise to thank the Lord for His great deliverance. Even the disciples (after their meal) sang a song of praise which was generally from Psalm 113-118 & 136.

Judaica Kiddush Cup

"After singing the Hallel, they went out to the Mount of Olives." Matthew 26:30

Let us now partake of the fourth and last cup.

בָּרוּךְ אַתָּה יְיָ אֱלֹהֵינוּ מֶלֶךְ הָעוֹלָם בּוֹרֵא פְּרִי הַגָּפֶן

LEADER: Baruch atah Adonai, Eloheynu Melech ha'olam, borey p'ri ha'gafen. Amen.

ALL: Blessed are You, O LORD our God, King of the Universe, Who creates the fruit of the vine. Amen.

(Take the fourth and final sip.)

HODU L'ADONAI – Give Thanks to the Lord

(To be sung in Hebrew and English. Additional translation in italics)

Hodu L'Adonai ki tov ki l'olam chasdo (repeat)

Hodu, hodu, hodu, hodu, hodu l'Adonai ki tov (repeat)

Hodu l'Elohey ha elohim ki l'olam chasdo (repeat) *(Give thanks to the God of gods.)*

Hodu, hodu, hodu, hodu, hodu l'Adonai ki tov (repeat)

Hodu l'Adonai ha adonim ki l'olam chasdo (repeat) *(Give thanks to the Lord of lords.)*

Hodu, hodu, hodu, hodu, hodu l'Adonai ki tov (repeat)

Give thanks to the LORD. He is Good. His Mercy endures forever. (repeat)

Oh Praise His Name and Worship Him. Give thanks to the LORD He is Good. (Repeat)

Nirtzah - Desire & Acceptance

LEADER: *Nirtzah* is the final act of the Seder. We have placed ourselves in the midst of our ancestors as this event unfolded before us. We pray this celebration finds acceptance in your hearts and may you desire it again next year, and every year, until Messiah comes back. May we gather again next year to celebrate this feast.

ALL: May Zion be blessed with peace, may His covenant people come to know Him as Lord and Messiah, and may all mankind someday live in harmony and contentment under His dominion. Amen.

LEADER: Every year at Passover, since the time that the Children of Israel were in exile, it has been traditional to say, "This year here, but next year, LORD willing, we will celebrate it in Jerusalem."

The return of our Messiah Yeshua is drawing near. When He comes, there will be a New Jerusalem as He establishes His Kingdom here on earth. May we all look forward to the day that we celebrate in the New Jerusalem.

לְשָׁנָה הַבָּאָה בִּירוּשָׁלָיִם

LA SHANA HABA AH B'YERUSHALAYIM - The Year to Come in Jerusalem

(To be sung in Hebrew. Translation in italics)

La Shana haba ah, La Shana haba ah
(The year to come, the year to come)

La Shana haba ah birushalayim
(The year to come in Jerusalem)

La Shana haba ah, La Shana haba ah
(The year to come, the year to come)

La Shana haba ah b'eretz Yisrael
(The year to come in the Land of Israel)

La Shana ha z'oht, La Shana ha z'oht
(That year, that year)

La Shana ha z'oht birushalayim
(That year in Jerusalem)

La Shana ha z'oht, La Shana ha z'oht
(That year, that year)

La Shana ha z'oht b'eretz Yisrael
(That year in the Land of Israel)

This concludes our Passover Seder.

Made in the USA
Middletown, DE
01 March 2019